The Gettysburg Address

D1368738

The Gettysburg Address

by ABRAHAM LINCOLN

Illustrated by Michael McCurdy

Foreword by Garry Wills

SCHOLASTIC INC.
NEW YORK TORONTO LONDON AUCKLAND SYDNEY

FOREWORD

During the first three days of July 1863, the Civil War armies of the North and South slaughtered each other in the fields surrounding the town of Gettysburg. By the evening of the third day, fifty thousand people were killed, wounded, or missing. General Robert E. Lee had to leave his dead on the field when he retreated to the South. The various states of the Union wanted to carry their dead back home to churchyards and family plots for burial, but the governor of Pennsylvania had to forbid this in order to prevent the spread of disease.

All the Northern states were asked to contribute to a common cemetery for the Gettysburg dead—a new exercise in cooperation. When it came time to dedicate the cemetery, the greatest orator of the time, Edward Everett, was asked to give a grand speech describing the battle and praising the Northern soldiers.

The president of the United States was also invited to speak at the formal opening of the gravesite. He would not deliver "the oration," according to the day's printed program; he would just make some brief "remarks." Abraham Lincoln prepared those remarks very carefully. Though he spoke for only three minutes, the crowd broke into applause five times. In 272 words he gave the battle a higher meaning. These men died, he said, to make Americans live up to their own beliefs—the belief in human equality, in the possibility of self-government. The pledge made by Americans in the Declaration of Independence had to be met—the pledge that "all men are created equal."

Lincoln's Gettysburg Address worked almost by magic, by incantation. It cast a spell. He held out a mystical vision of the spirit that should breathe through all our laws. It is the best example in history of the fact that nothing is more practical than idealism, that ideas matter, that words are more important than weapons.

Not only the Battle of Gettysburg, but the whole Civil War, means to us today what Lincoln said it must mean at that dark time of mourning for the dead. The nation, he believed, could be reborn out of those deaths; and it was.

—GARRY WILLS

Four score and seven years ago our fathers
brought forth on this continent, a new nation,

conceived in Liberty, and dedicated to the
proposition that all men are created equal.

Now we are engaged in a great civil war,
testing whether that nation, or any nation
so conceived and so dedicated, can long endure.

We are met on a great battle-field of that war.

We have come to dedicate a portion of that field,
as a final resting place for those who here

gave their lives that that nation might live.

It is altogether fitting and proper that we should do this.

But, in a larger sense, we can not dedicate—

we can not consecrate—we can not hallow—this ground.

The brave men, living and dead, who struggled here, have consecrated it, far above our poor power to add or detract.

The world will little note, nor long remember what we say here, but it can never forget what they did here.

It is for us the living, rather, to be dedicated here to the unfinished work which they who fought here have thus far so nobly advanced.

It is rather for us to be here dedicated to the great task remaining before us—that from these honored dead we take increased devotion to that cause for which they gave the last full measure of devotion—

that we here highly resolve that these dead
shall not have died in vain—that this nation, under God,
shall have a new birth of freedom—and that government
of the people, by the people, for the people,
shall not perish from the earth.

AFTERWORD

The drawings for this book were exciting to create. They sprang directly from my fascination with the Civil War—and with Abraham Lincoln. The Civil War was a devastating period in our country's history, and Abraham Lincoln was probably the most fascinating president we have ever had. I wanted my drawings to reflect the great dark struggle he and other Americans went through at that time.

The battles of Gettysburg and Antietam are of special interest to me, for at least one of my ancestors took part in these famous battles. One of my great-grandfathers, a Yankee named John Kenning, kept a journal throughout the war. Army Private John "Jack" Kenning was born in 1838 and was a cannoneer in the Independent Battery F, Pennsylvania Light Artillery. His name can be found on the Pennsylvania monument at Gettysburg. Jack left Pittsburgh in October 1861 to join what he called "The War of the Rebellion." He was a cabinetmaker by trade, and the family story is that he lost part of a thumb in a Civil War battle. Worse, he lost one of his best friends at Gettysburg, a man by the name of Jim Barrett.

Being in the artillery required more skill than being in the infantry. A cannoneer worked as part of a team, loading and firing cannons with shot, shell, or canister. Such a complex task required coordination and agility. Although the artillery took occasional hits, Great-grandfather Jack was probably safer among the big guns than he would have been farther down the field, fighting hand-to-hand in the infantry. Short, wiry, and fleet of foot, Great-grandfather Jack escaped the gunfire aimed at taller men and lived to tell the tale. He mustered out of the army in October 1864 and died in 1920 at the age of eighty-two.

When I made these drawings, I had my Great-grandfather Jack in mind. I never knew him, of course, any more than I knew Abraham Lincoln. But in creating these illustrations for Lincoln's greatest speech, I felt I was closer to the men of the Civil War than I had ever been.

—MICHAEL McCURDY

The so-called Bliss text, the last from Lincoln's hand,
is the text used for this book.

ISBN 0-590-93743-X

Illustrations and Afterword copyright © 1995 by Michael McCurdy.
Foreword by Garry Wills copyright © 1995 by Houghton Mifflin Company.
All rights reserved. Published by Scholastic Inc., 555 Broadway, New York, NY 10012, by arrangement with Houghton Mifflin Company.

12 11 10 9 8 7 6 5 4 3   7 8 9/9 0 1 2/0

Printed in the U.S.A.   08
First Scholastic printing, February 1997

Hand set and machine set in Monotype Bulmer series 462
by Firefly Press.